Introductic

Quick & Easy Baby Quilts is a collection of baby and toddler quilts with endless options. There are nine timeless patterns you will use again and again. You'll find beautiful quilts that you can make in a timely manner without sacrificing design or tradition.

These stylish and trendy baby quilts will be your source for the special keepsake quilts you want to make, and you will find optional fabric choices included. It's not only the blocks and piecing that determine the final look, but the fabric choices too. A single pattern can look unrecognizable when the fabrics are changed.

Sometimes a quilter needs a little help visualizing other fabric and color choices in a quilt pattern, and you'll find that help in this book. Changing fabrics gives you possibilities to personalize and create the perfect keepsake for a special bundle of joy. This is the only book you'll ever need when planning those special quilts.

Enjoy!

Table of Contents

Rose Wall Quilt, *page 16*

Choo! Choo!, *page 8*

Road to Bedtime, *page 37*

Dotty Scotty

The classic Scotty Dog block is always in style. This easy-to-piece block pattern can be made in a day or two, and can easily be made appropriate for a boy or a girl.

Designed & Quilted by Chris Malone

Skill Level
Confident Beginner

Finished Size
Quilt Size: 40" x 49½"
Block Size: 8" x 8" finished
Number of Blocks: 12

Materials
- ¼ yard red-with-black dots
- ⅓ yard black-with-red dots
- ⅝ yard black-and-white with red dots
- ⅝ yard white-with-black dots
- ¾ yard red-on-red dots
- 1 yard black solid
- Backing to size
- Batting to size
- Thread
- White and black pearl cotton
- Basic sewing tools and supplies

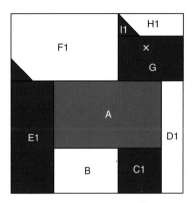

Black Dotty Scotty
8" x 8" Finished Block
Make 8

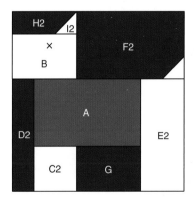

White Dotty Scotty
8" x 8" Finished Block
Make 4

Cutting

From red-with-black dots:
- Cut 1 (5½" by fabric width) strip.
  Subcut strip into 12 (3½" x 5½") A rectangles.

From black-with-red dots:
- Cut 1 (2" by fabric width) strip.
  Subcut strip into 20 (2") K squares.
- Cut 1 (5½" by fabric width) strip.
  Subcut strip into 4 (5½") N squares.

From black-and-white with red dots:
- Cut 2 (8½" by fabric width) strips.
  Subcut strips into 31 (2" x 8½") J strips.

From white-with-black dots:
- Cut 2 (5½" by fabric width) strips.
    Subcut strips into 4 (2½" x 5½") E2 rectangles,
    8 each 3½" x 5½" F1 and 1½" x 5½"
    D1 rectangles, 4 (2½") C2 squares and
    8 (1½") I2 squares.
- Cut 1 (3½" by fabric width) strip.
    Subcut strip into 12 (2½" x 3½") B rectangles
    and 8 (1½" x 3½") H1 rectangles.

From red-on-red dots:
- Cut 4 (5½" by fabric width) strips.
    Trim strips to make 2 (5½" x 40") L strips and
    2 (5½" x 30½") M strips.

From black solid:
- Cut 1 (5½" by fabric width) strip.
    Subcut strip into 8 (2½" x 5½") E1 rectangles
    and 4 each 3½" x 5½" F2 and 1½" x 5½"
    D2 rectangles.
- Cut 1 (1½" by fabric width) strip.
    Subcut strip into 16 (1½") I1 squares.
- Cut 1 (3½" by fabric width) strip.
    Subcut strip into 12 (2½" x 3½") G rectangles
    and 4 (1½" x 3½") H2 rectangles.
- Cut 1 (2½" by fabric width) strip.
    Subcut strip into 8 (2½") C1 squares.
- Cut 5 (2¼" by fabric width) binding strips.

Completing the Blocks

1. Draw a diagonal line from corner to corner on the wrong side of each I1 and I2 square.

2. To complete one Black Dotty Scotty block, select one each A, B, C1, D1, E1, F1, G and H1 piece, and two I1 squares.

3. Referring to Figure 1, place a marked I1 square right sides together on one corner of F1 and stitch on the marked line. Trim seam allowance to ¼" and press I1 to the right side to complete an F-I unit.

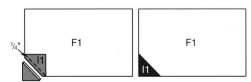

Figure 1

4. Repeat step 3 with I1 on one end of H1 to make an H-I unit as shown in Figure 2.

Figure 2

5. Sew the H-I unit to G and add the F-I unit to make the head unit as shown in Figure 3; press.

Figure 3

6. Sew B to C1 and add A; press. Add D1 to the A-C1 side and E1 to the A-B side to complete the body/legs unit as shown in Figure 4; press.

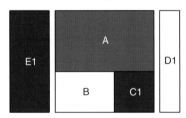

Figure 4

7. Join the head and body/legs units to complete one Black Dotty Scotty block referring to Figure 5; press.

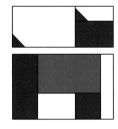

Figure 5

8. Using white pearl cotton, cross-stitch an X (see stitch diagram) for an eye on the G rectangle 1¾" from outer edge and ½" down from seam between H1 and G as shown in Figure 6.

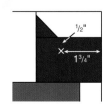

Figure 6

Individual Cross Stitch

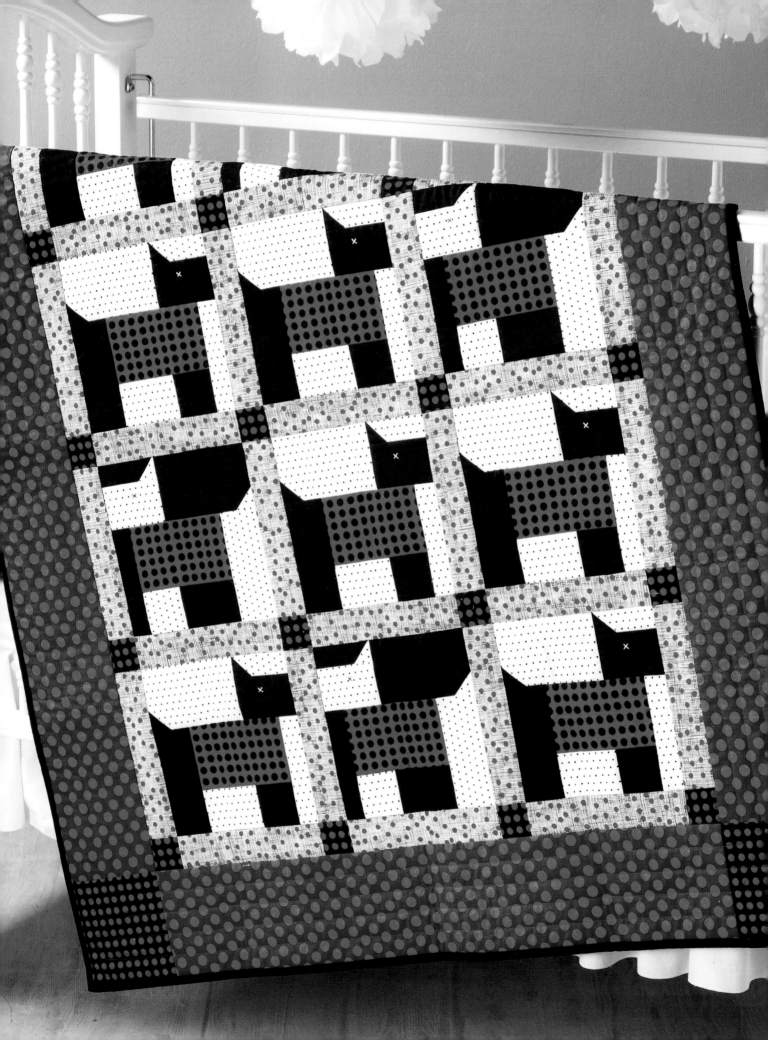

9. Repeat steps 2–8 to complete a total of 8 Black Dotty Scotty blocks.

10. Repeat steps 2–8 with A, B, C2, D2, E2, F2, G, H2 and I2 pieces, adding the cross-stitched X for eye using black pearl cotton, to complete four White Dotty Scotty blocks referring to Figure 7.

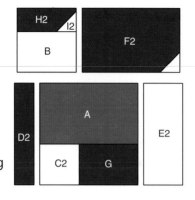

Figure 7

Completing the Quilt Top
Refer to the Assembly Diagram for positioning of blocks.

1. Arrange and join one White Dotty Scotty block with two Black Dotty Scotty blocks and four J strips to make a block row; press. Repeat to make four block rows, moving the blocks around in each row.

2. Join three J strips with four K squares to make a sashing row; press. Repeat to make a total of five sashing rows.

3. Join the sashing rows with the block rows to complete the quilt center; press.

Dotty Scotty
Assembly Diagram 40" x 49½"

4. Sew the L strips to opposite long sides of the quilt center; press.

5. Sew an N square to each end of each M strip; press. Sew the M-N strips to the top and bottom of the quilt center to complete the quilt top.

Completing the Quilt

1. Sandwich the batting between the pieced top and a prepared backing piece; baste layers together. Quilt as desired.

2. When quilting is complete remove basting; trim batting and backing fabric even with raw edges of the pieced top.

3. Prepare binding and stitch to quilt front edges, matching raw edges, mitering corners and overlapping ends. Fold binding to back side and stitch in place to finish. ●

Your Way

If you're looking for a great project to use up leftover fabrics, consider Dotty Scotty. Sort your fabrics and plan each block differently—the scrappier the better.

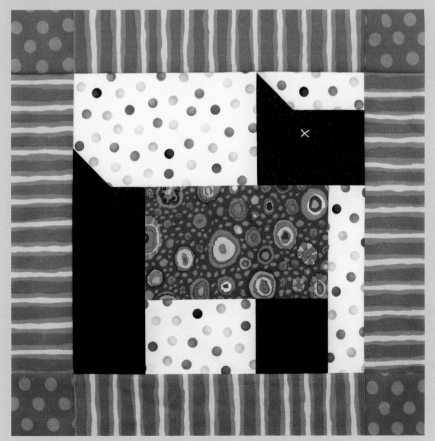

Choo! Choo!

Beautiful quilts don't have to be difficult to be spectacular.
This is a perfect example of how simple piecing and appliqué
can make a quilt that will be treasured for years to come.

Design by Gina Gempesaw
Quilted by Carole Whaling

Skill Level
Confident Beginner

Finished Size
Quilt Size: 56" x 56"
Block Size: 9" x 7½" finished
Number of Blocks: 20

Materials
- 15 assorted bright-color fat eighths
- ⅝ yard red tonal
- 2⅔ yards white solid
- Backing to size
- Batting to size
- Thread
- ½ yard fusible web
- Template material
- Basic sewing tools and supplies

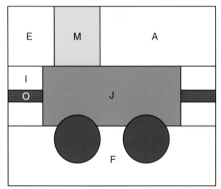

Train 1
9" x 7½" Finished Block
Make 3

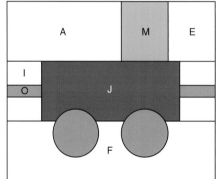

Train 1 Reversed
9" x 7½" Finished Block
Make 2

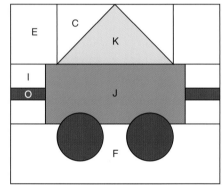

Train 2
9" x 7½" Finished Block
Make 5

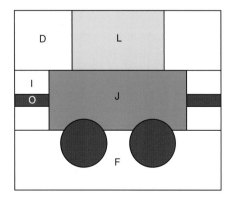

Train 3
9" x 7½" Finished Block
Make 5

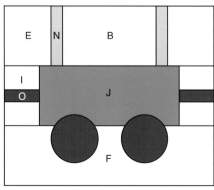

Train 4
9" x 7½" Finished Block
Make 5

Cutting

Prepare template for the wheel using the pattern given on the pattern insert. Prepare the wheel circles for fusible appliqué, cutting from fabric as listed in cutting instructions, on the pattern and referring to Raw-Edge Fusible Appliqué on page 15.

Each train row is made with three different fabrics—one for the train body, one for the top sections and one for the wheels and the links. Sort the fat eighths into five sets of three, assigning each fabric positioning in the blocks before cutting.

From each set of 3 assorted bright-color fat eighths:

- Cut 1 (6½" x 21") strip from train body fabric.
  Subcut strip into 4 (3" x 6½") J rectangles and 6 (2½") R squares.
- Cut 1 (5½" x 21") strip from the top section fabric.
  Subcut strip into 1 each 3" x 5½" K, 3" x 4½" L and 2½" x 3" M rectangle, 2 (1" x 3") N rectangles and 8 (2½") R squares.
- Cut 1 (1" x 21") O strip from the links/wheels fabric.
- Prepare 8 wheel circles for fusible appliqué using the links/wheels fabric.

From remainder of 15 assorted bright-color fat eighths:

- Cut 30 (2½") assorted R squares (to total 100 R squares).

From red tonal:

- Cut 6 (2¼" by fabric width) binding strips.

From white solid:

- Cut 7 (3" by fabric width) strips.
  Subcut strips into 10 (3" x 9½") F rectangles, 5 (3" x 5½") A rectangles, 5 (3" x 4½") B rectangles, 20 (3") C/D squares (separate for 10 each C and D squares) and 25 (2½" x 3") E rectangles.
- Cut 5 (2" by fabric width) strips.
  Trim strips to make 5 (2" x 36½") G strips.
- Cut 2 (9½" by fabric width) strips.
  Subcut strips into 5 (9½") H squares and 10 (3" x 9½") F rectangles (to total 20 F rectangles).
- Cut 5 (1½" by fabric width) strips.
  Subcut strips to make 10 (1½" x 21") I strips.
- Cut 5 (2" by fabric width) P/Q strips.
- Cut 6 (2½" by fabric width) S/T strips.

Here's a Tip

Pin matching pieces together for each row after cutting for ease of piecing. For example, keep the eight matching wheel pieces together with the J, K, L, M and N circles and I-O link units cut for the blocks in row 1. When making the Train 1 block in the row, select the pieces from the set needed for that block. After stitching, keep the completed block together with the unstitched pieces until all blocks in the row are stitched.

Completing the Links Units

1. Select one O strip and two I strips. Sew the O strip between the I strips with right sides together along the 21" edges to make an I-O strip set; press. Subcut the strip set into eight 2" x 3" I-O link units as shown in Figure 1.

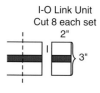

I-O Link Unit
Cut 8 each set

Figure 1

2. Repeat step 1 with the remaining I and O strips to make a total of five different I-O strip sets, subcutting each strip set into eight matching I-O link units.

Completing the Train 1 Blocks

1. To complete one Train 1 block, select one each A, E, F, J and M rectangle and two each matching I-O link units and prepared wheel circles.

2. Sew E to M to A to make the top row as shown in Figure 2; press.

Figure 2

3. Sew an I-O link unit to opposite ends of the J rectangle to make the center row as shown in Figure 3; press.

Figure 3

4. Sew the top and center rows together and add F as shown in Figure 4; press.

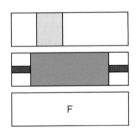

Figure 4

5. Fuse and stitch the wheel circles to the stitched unit ½" up from the seam between F and J, and ½" from the seams between J and the I-O link units as shown in Figure 5.

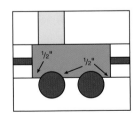

Figure 5

6. Repeat steps 1–5 to complete a total of three Train 1 blocks, one for each of three rows.

7. Repeat steps 1–5 to complete two Train 1 Reversed blocks, one for each of two rows, referring to Figure 6.

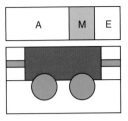

Figure 6

Completing the Train 2 Blocks

1. To complete one Train 2 block, select one each F, J and K rectangle, two each matching I-O link units and prepared wheel circles, and two each C squares and E rectangles.

2. Draw a diagonal line from corner to corner on the wrong side of each C square.

3. Referring to Figure 7, place a C square right sides together on one end of K and stitch on the marked line. Trim seam allowance to ¼" and press C to the right side. Repeat on the opposite end of K to complete a C-K unit.

Figure 7

4. Sew E to each end of the C-K unit to make the top row as shown in Figure 8; press.

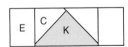

Figure 8

5. Repeat steps 3–5 for Completing the Train 1 Blocks to complete one Train 2 block as shown in Figure 9; press.

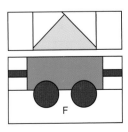

Figure 9

6. Repeat steps 1–5 to complete a total of five Train 2 blocks.

Completing the Train 3 Blocks

1. To complete one Train 3 block, select one each L, F and J rectangle, two D squares and two each matching I-O link units and prepared wheel circles.

2. Sew a D square to each end of L to make the top row as shown in Figure 10; press.

Figure 10

3. Repeat steps 3–5 for Completing the Train 1 Blocks to complete one Train 3 block as shown in Figure 11; press.

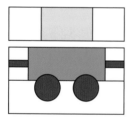

Figure 11

4. Repeat steps 1–3 to complete a total of five Train 3 blocks.

Completing the Train 4 Blocks

1. To complete one Train 4 block, select one each B, F and J rectangle, two each E and N rectangles and two each matching I-O link units and prepared wheel circles.

2. Sew N to each end of B and add E to each N side to complete the top row as shown in Figure 12; press.

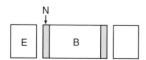

Figure 12

3. Repeat steps 3–5 for Completing the Train 1 Blocks to complete one Train 4 block as shown in Figure 13; press.

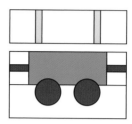

Figure 13

4. Repeat steps 1–3 to complete a total of five Train 4 blocks.

Completing the Quilt Top

Refer to the Assembly Diagram when joining blocks and H squares to make the rows.

1. Select a matching set of Train 1, 2, 3 and 4 blocks and join to make a train row as shown in Figure 14; press.

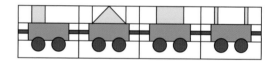

Figure 14

2. Sew a G strip to the top of the train row; press.

3. Sew an H square to the left end to make Row 1 as shown in Figure 15; press.

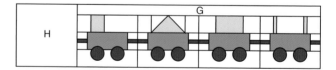

Figure 15

4. Repeat steps 1–3 to make Rows 3 and 5, altering the placement of Train 2, 3 and 4 blocks as desired.

5. Repeat steps 1–3, adding the H square to the right end of the train row and using the Train 1 Reversed blocks to complete Rows 2 and 4.

6. Join the rows to complete the quilt center; press.

7. Join the P/Q strips on the short ends to make one long strip; press. Subcut strip into two each 2" x 45½" P strips and 2" x 48½" Q strips.

8. Sew P strips to opposite sides and Q strips to the top and bottom of the quilt center; press.

9. Join 24 assorted R squares to make a pieced side strip; press. Repeat to make a second side strip. Sew these strips to opposite sides of the quilt center; press.

10. Repeat step 9 with 26 R squares to make a pieced strip; press. Repeat to make a second pieced strip. Sew the pieced strips to the top and bottom of the quilt center.

11. Join the S/T strips on the short ends to make a long strip; press. Subcut strip into two each 2½" x 52½" S strips and 2½" x 56½" T strips.

12. Sew S strips to opposite sides and T strips to the top and bottom to complete the quilt top; press.

Completing the Quilt

1. Sandwich the batting between the pieced top and a prepared backing piece; baste layers together. Quilt as desired.

2. When quilting is complete remove basting; trim batting and backing fabric even with raw edges of the pieced top.

3. Prepare binding and stitch to quilt front edges, matching raw edges, mitering corners and overlapping ends. Fold binding to back side and stitch in place to finish. ●

Designer's Quote

"I love making quilts with simple shapes for babies. Trains are so enjoyed by everyone that a baby quilt with trains on it, done with simple shapes, is just delightful!" —Gina Gempesaw

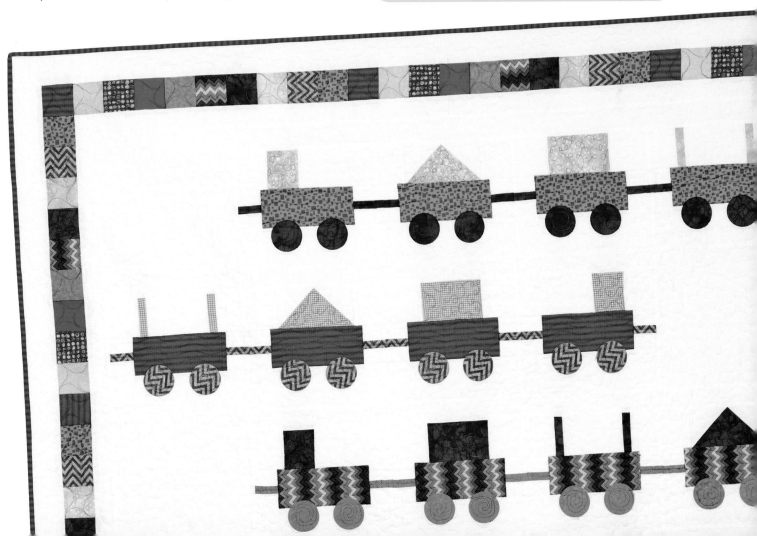

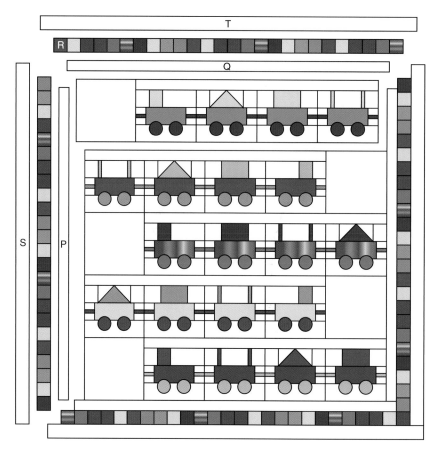

Choo! Choo!
Assembly Diagram 56" x 56"

Your Way

If brights aren't what you're looking for in a baby quilt, why not try a soft palette of aqua, gray and white? This simple train can be stitched in any color combination.

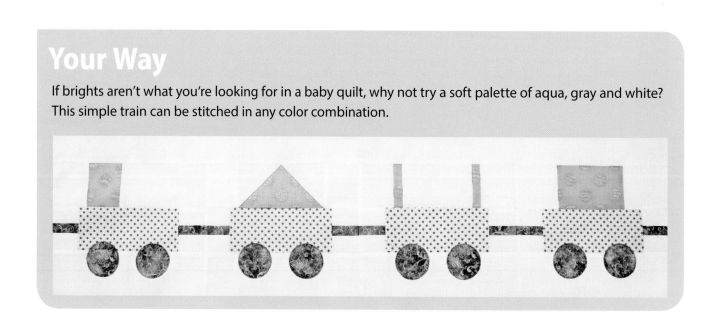

Raw-Edge Fusible Appliqué

One of the easiest ways to appliqué is the fusible-web method. Paper-backed fusible web motifs are fused to the wrong side of fabric, cut out and then fused to a foundation fabric and stitched in place by hand or machine. You can use this method for raw- or turned-edge appliqué.

1. If the appliqué motif is directional, it should be reversed for raw-edge fusible appliqué. If doing several identical appliqué motifs, trace reversed motif shapes onto template material to make reusable templates.

2. Use templates or trace the appliqué motif shapes onto paper side of paper-backed fusible web. Leave at least ½" between shapes. Cut out shapes leaving a margin around traced lines.

3. Follow manufacturer's instructions and fuse shapes to wrong side of fabric as indicated on pattern for color and number to cut.

4. Cut out appliqué shapes on traced lines and remove paper backing from fusible web.

5. Again following manufacturer's instructions, arrange and fuse pieces on the foundation fabric referring to appliqué motif included in pattern.

6. Hand- or machine-stitch around edges. *Note: Position a light- to medium-weight stabilizer behind the appliqué motif to keep the fabric from puckering during machine stitching. Some stitch possibilities are satin or zigzag, blanket or running stitch.*

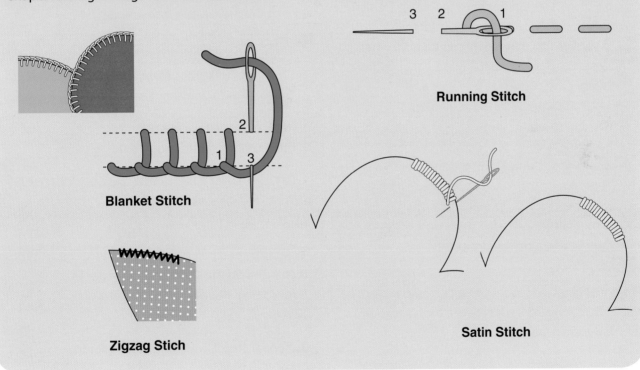

Running Stitch

Blanket Stitch

Zigzag Stich

Satin Stitch

Rose Wall Quilt

Any little girl would love this beautiful wall hanging. It's a fast and easy project that will be the focus of any room it's placed in.

Designed & Quilted by Missy Shepler

Skill Level
Confident Beginner

Finished Size
Quilt Size: 40" x 40"

Materials
- 3 (10" x 8") rectangles green tonals for outer petals and leaves
- 3 (10" x 6") rectangles pink/burgundy fabrics for inner petals and flower centers
- ⅛ yard each 3 different green tonals for stems
- ½ yard each 6 different light to dark pink/rose/cream prints
- ½ yard burgundy tonal for binding
- Backing to size
- Batting to size
- 3 each 5" x 8" and 5" x 6" batting rectangles
- Thread
- No. 5 pearl cotton to match flower center fabrics
- Basic sewing tools and supplies

Project Note: *When selecting fabrics for this project, be sure there is some contrast between the background and flower/stem fabrics.*

Cutting
Prepare templates for inner and outer petals, flower center and leaf using patterns given on the insert. Cut as per Making 3-D Leaves & Flowers (page 18).

From 3 green tonals:
- Cut 1 (1½" x 22½") short stem strip.
- Cut 1 (1½" x 27½") mid-length stem strip.
- Cut 1 (1½" x 30½") long stem strip.

From 6 pink/rose/cream prints:
- Cut 2 (5½" by fabric width) strips each fabric. Subcut strips into 30 (2½" x 5½") rectangles each fabric (180 total). **Note:** *Extra rectangles are cut to allow for moving them around as you stitch.*

From burgundy tonal:
- Cut 5 (2¼" by fabric width) binding strips.

Completing the Quilt Background
Refer to the Assembly Diagram for positioning of pieces.

1. Arrange and join eight pink/rose rectangles on the short ends to make an A row; press. Repeat to make a total of 10 A rows.

2. Repeat step 1 with nine rectangles to make 10 B rows.

3. Sew an A row to a B row, centering the A row on the B row as shown in Figure 1; press. Repeat with all A and B rows.

Figure 1

Making 3-D Flowers & Leaves

1. Fold the 10" x 8" green tonal rectangles in half with right sides together to make 5" x 8" rectangles.

2. Trace one outer petal and two leaf shapes on each folded rectangle, leaving ½" between traced shapes (Figure A).

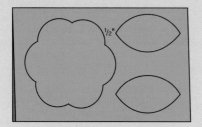

Figure A

3. Place each traced rectangle on a 5" x 8" batting rectangle; sew along traced lines through all layers, pivoting at corners and leaving a 1½" opening on each shape (Figure B).

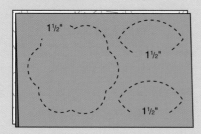

Figure B

4. Cut the stitched shapes apart. Trim batting close to seam. Trim excess fabric ⅛"–¼" from stitched seam. Clip into curves (Figure C).

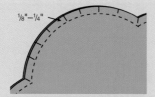

Figure C

5. Turn shapes right side out; press edges flat at seams.

6. Tuck seam allowances to the inside at opening edges; hand-stitch opening edges closed (Figure D).

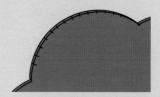

Figure D

7. Repeat all steps using the 10" x 6" pink/burgundy rectangles and 5" x 6" batting rectangles to complete the inner petals and flower centers, tracing one inner petal and one flower center on each folded rectangle.

8. Center a flower center on each inner petal shape; hand-stitch in place in the center or around outer edges. *Note: The flower is more secure if the whole edge is stitched down, but it is not necessary to do this if the project will be used as a wall quilt.*

9. Center a stitched center/inner petal unit on each outer petal shape and stitch in place as in step 8.

10. Using a chain stitch and pearl cotton, hand-stitch vein lines in leaves as marked on pattern.

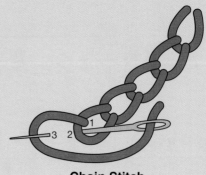

Chain Stitch

11. Repeat step 10 on the inner petal piece next to the edges of the flower center, stitching through the inner and outer petals (Figure E).

Figure E

12. After quilting is complete, arrange and hand-stitch one flower and two leaves at the top of each stem, stitching the tips of the leaf motifs in place first and then adding the flower motifs on top as shown in Figure F. ***Note:*** *You may stitch the motifs in place all around instead of leaving edges free, if desired.*

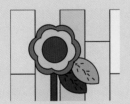

Figure F

4. Join the A-B rows as in step 3, with ends of B rows extending beyond the ends of the A rows.

5. Trim excess from the top and bottom of the B rows even with the top and bottom of the A rows to complete the quilt background referring to Figure 2.

Figure 2

Adding the Stems

1. Fold each stem strip in half along length with wrong sides together; stitch along the long raw edges using a scant ¼" seam allowance. Press folded edge flat.

2. Referring to Figure 3, place the long stem strip on the quilt background in the middle position, starting with one end at the bottom edge and referring to the Assembly Diagram for positioning on the background strips; pin in place.

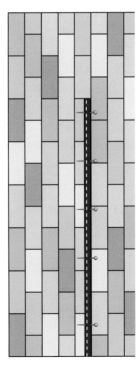

Figure 3

3. Stitch in place just inside the previously stitched seam as shown in Figure 4.

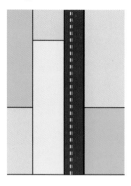

Figure 4

4. Press the folded edge of the stem strip over the seam and seam allowance and hand-stitch the folded edge in place referring to Figure 5.

Figure 5

5. Repeat steps 2–4 with the remaining stem strips referring to the Assembly Diagram for positioning.

Completing the Quilt

1. Sandwich the batting between the pieced top and a prepared backing piece; baste layers together. Quilt as desired.

2. When quilting is complete remove basting and trim batting and backing fabric even with raw edges of the pieced top.

3. Prepare binding and stitch to quilt front edges, matching raw edges, mitering corners and overlapping ends. Fold binding to back side and stitch in place.

4. Prepare six leaves and three flowers referring to Making 3-D Flowers & Leaves sidebar, using the 10" x 8" and 10" x 6" fabric rectangles and the 5" x 8" and 5" x 6" batting rectangles with the prepared templates.

5. Arrange and hand-stitch a set of two leaves and one flower at the top of each stem, stitching the leaves first and the flowers on top to finish. ●

Your Way

Not every nursery has to be pink or blue. Today's trends lean toward the unusual. Why not use blacks and whites with pops of red?

Making Appliquéd Flowers

Three-dimensional flowers are not appropriate for use on a crib quilt as they pose a choking hazard. However, the flowers can be easily changed from 3-D to one-dimensional flowers and machine-appliquéd in place. Use fusible web and follow the manufacturer's instructions to transfer the pattern shapes given for the 3-D method to the fabrics. Fuse the shapes to the background at the end of the stems, layering the pieces in the same order as for the 3-D version. Stitch around the shapes using your favorite machine-appliqué stitches to secure the pieces in place.

Rose Wall Quilt
Assembly Diagram 40" x 40"

Tutti Frutti

Create a unique big-block quilt that you can easily piece in a day.
The extra-large pieces make this an easy project yet very trendy.

Designed & Quilted by Robin Waggoner

Skill Level

Confident Beginner

Finished Size

Quilt Size: 39½" x 39½"

Materials

- 1 fat quarter each light pink, light blue, light orange and light green solids
- ½ yard each red, dark blue, dark orange and dark green solids
- ⅝ yard white solid
- ⅞ yard gray solid
- Backing to size
- Batting to size
- Thread
- Basic sewing tools and supplies

Cutting

From each light solid fat quarter:

- Cut 1 (7⅞" x 21") strip.
  Subcut strip into 1 (7⅞") B square each fabric (4 total).
- Cut 1 (7½" x 21") strip.
  Subcut strip into 2 (7½") A squares each fabric (8 total).

From red & dark blue solids:

- Cut 1 (11⅛" by fabric width) strip each fabric. Subcut each strip into 1 (11⅛") C square and 1 (7⅞") B square each fabric. Cut the C squares on both diagonals to make 4 C triangles each fabric. Set aside 2 C triangles each fabric for your scrap basket.

From dark orange & dark green solids:

- Cut 1 (11⅛" by fabric width) strip each fabric. Subcut each strip into 1 (11⅛") C square and 2 (7⅞") B squares each fabric. Cut the C squares on both diagonals to make 4 C triangles each fabric. Set aside 2 triangles each fabric for your scrap basket.

From white solid:

- Cut 1 (7⅞" by fabric width) strip.
  Subcut strip into 2 (7⅞") D squares.
- Cut 1 (7½" by fabric width) strip.
  Subcut strip into 4 (7½") E squares.

From gray solid:

- Cut 1 (11⅛" by fabric width) strip.
  Subcut strip into 2 (11⅛") squares. Cut each square on both diagonals to make 8 F triangles.
- Cut 5 (2¼" by fabric width) binding strips.

Completing the Quilt Top

Refer to the Assembly Diagram for positioning of pieces for all steps.

1. Mark a diagonal line from corner to corner on the wrong side of a light pink B square. Place right sides together with a red B square and stitch ¼" from each side of the marked line. Cut apart on the marked line to make two B units as shown in Figure 1.

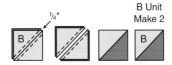

Figure 1

2. Repeat step 1 with light blue/dark blue, light orange/dark orange and light green/dark green B squares to make two B triangle units in each color combination as shown in Figure 2.

B Units
Make 2 each

Figure 2

3. Repeat step 1 with D squares and dark green and dark orange B squares to make two each green and orange B-D units as shown in Figure 3.

B-D Units
Make 2 each

Figure 3

4. Arrange and join the B and B-D units with the A and E squares, and C and F triangles in diagonal rows referring to the Assembly Diagram; press seams in adjoining rows in opposite directions.

5. Join the pieced diagonal rows to complete the quilt top; press.

Here's a Tip

Try using the right and wrong sides of print fabrics for the darks and lights in each color family to produce an interesting quilt.

Tutti Frutti
Assembly Diagram 39½" x 39½"

Completing the Quilt

1. Sandwich the batting between the pieced top and a prepared backing piece; baste layers together. Quilt as desired.

2. When quilting is complete remove basting; trim batting and backing fabric even with raw edges of the pieced top.

3. Prepare binding and stitch to quilt front edges, matching raw edges, mitering corners and overlapping ends. Fold binding to back side and stitch in place to finish. ●

Designer's Quote

"I was inspired by the play of the colors and how the lights and darks give the illusion of transparency." —Robin Waggoner

Your Way

Adding a brighter palette of four colors with coordinating prints is another option that is well suited for this pattern.

Neopolitan Baby

Believe it or not, this lovely Orange Peel–block quilt can be done in a weekend. It's a simple technique with raw edges that will fray when washed, leaving it with a soft and cuddly fringe.

Designed & Quilted by CJ Behling

Skill Level
Confident Beginner

Finished Size
Quilt Size: 49" x 58"
Block Size: 9" x 9" finished
Number of Blocks: 30

Materials
- 16 assorted flannel fat quarters—4 each pinks, greens, yellows and grays
- ⅝ yard gray flannel
- 2½ yards cream flannel
- Backing to size
- Batting to size
- Thread
- Basic sewing tools and supplies

Cutting
Prepare template for the petal shape using pattern given on insert. Cut as per pattern and instructions. Transfer dots to petals after cutting.

From flannel fat quarters:
- Cut petals as per pattern for a total of 120 petals (30 each color). Transfer dots at points on pattern to each petal.
- Cut 8 (2½" x 6½") B rectangles each color from the remainder of the yellow and gray fat quarters.
- Cut 10 (2½" x 6½") C rectangles each color from the remainder of the green and pink fat quarters.

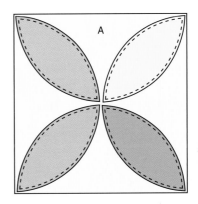

Orange Peel
9" x 9" Finished Block
Make 30

From gray flannel:
- Cut 6 (2½" by fabric width) binding strips.

From cream flannel:
- Cut 8 (10" by fabric width) strips.
  Subcut strips into 30 (10") A squares.

Completing the Blocks
1. To complete one block, select one A square and 4 petal pieces, one of each color.

2. Fold the A square in half and then in half again and crease to divide into four quarters as shown in Figure 1.

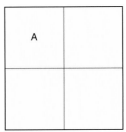

Figure 1

3. Place a pink petal piece in the upper left quarter with one point about 1/16" from the center of the square and the remaining point at the upper left corner as shown in Figure 2; pin to hold.

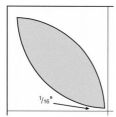

Figure 2

4. Stitch 1/8" from edge of petal all around to secure using marked dots as guides as shown in Figure 3. **Note:** *Raw edges remain unstitched and allowed to fray.*

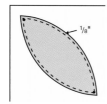

Figure 3

5. Continue adding petals in the same manner in a clockwise direction beginning with yellow, then green and then gray.

6. Square the block to 9½" x 9½", centering the petals in the trimmed square to complete one Orange Peel block.

7. Repeat steps 1–6 to complete a total of 30 Orange Peel blocks.

Here's a Tip

Cut binding strips 2½" instead of the usual 2¼" to accommodate the thickness of the flannel at the edges.

Completing the Quilt Top

Refer to the Assembly Diagram when piecing the quilt top.

1. Arrange and join five blocks to make a row, keeping the petal edges out of the seams when stitching by pinning or pushing excess away from the seam as you stitch; press.

2. Repeat step 1 to make six rows.

3. Join the rows to complete the quilt center; press.

4. Join the yellow B rectangles on the short ends to make one long strip; press. Trim the strip to 2½" x 45½". Repeat with the gray B rectangles.

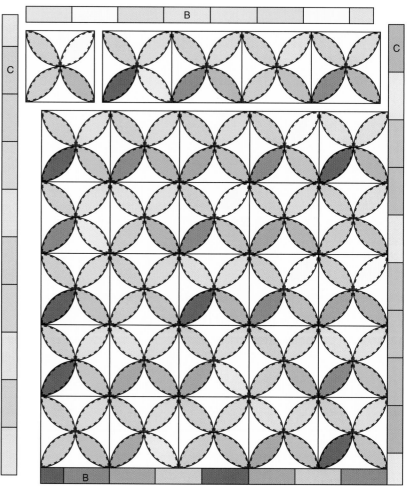

Neapolitan Baby
Assembly Diagram 49" x 58"

5. Sew the B strips to the top and bottom of the quilt center; press.

6. Repeat step 4 with the pink and green C rectangles to make two 2½" x 58½" C strips.

7. Sew a C strip to opposite long sides of the quilt center to complete the quilt top; press.

Completing the Quilt

1. Sandwich the batting between the pieced top and a prepared backing piece; baste layers together. Quilt as desired.

2. When quilting is complete remove basting; trim batting and backing fabric even with raw edges of the pieced top.

3. Prepare binding and stitch to quilt front edges, matching raw edges, mitering corners and overlapping ends. Fold binding to back side and stitch in place to finish. ●

Designer's Quote

"I noticed my 5½-month-old granddaughter River's intense interest when I placed her on a quilt on the floor. She focused on the assorted colors and patterns. I played with some textures and found that the texture and color held her focus and attention while her mom and I enjoyed a nice long visit." —CJ Behling

Your Way

This Orange Peel block can be made in any color combination. It's an easy pattern to adapt to a room theme and make it fit. Another fun idea would be to use different textured fabrics such as minky.

Rocking on the Water

This easy pattern only requires a fun novelty fabric and a couple of coordinating colors to make it a treasured keepsake. Throw in the adorable matching pillow and you have a nursery theme.

Designed & Quilted by Connie Kauffman

Skill Level
Confident Beginner

Finished Sizes
Quilt Size: 38" x 56"
Pillow Size: 11" x 11"

Materials
- Scrap black solid
- ⅜ yard white tonal
- ⅝ yard light gray tonal
- ⅝ yard white whale print
- ¾ yard dark gray tonal
- 2⅛ yards blue tonal
- 15"-square lining for pillow
- Backing to size for quilt
- 15"-square batting for pillow
- Batting to size for quilt
- Thread
- Polyester fiberfill
- ¼ yard fusible web
- Template material
- Basic sewing tools and supplies

Cutting
Prepare templates for whale shapes using patterns given on insert. Cut as per patterns and instructions.

From white tonal:
- Cut 1 (9½" by fabric width) strip.
    Subcut strip into 2 (9½") squares for pillow form and 1 (7½") I square.

From light gray tonal:
- Cut 2 (3⅞" by fabric width) strips.
    Subcut strips into 8 (3⅞") G squares, 4 (3⅞") J squares and 20 (1½") D squares. Cut the G squares in half on 1 diagonal to make 16 G triangles.
- Cut 5 (1½" by fabric width) strips.
    Subcut strips into 140 (1½") D squares (160 total).

From white whale print:
- Cut 4 (4½" by fabric width) strips.
    Subcut strips into 28 (4½") A squares and 2 each 1½" x 7½" K strips and 1½" x 9½" L strips.

From dark gray tonal:
- Cut 5 (4½" by fabric width) strips.
    Subcut strips into 67 (2½" x 4½") B rectangles.

From blue tonal:
- Cut 3 (2½" by fabric width) strips.
    Subcut strips into 40 (2½") C squares.
- Cut 5 (6½" by fabric width) strips.
    Trim 2 strips to make 2 (6½" x 26½") H strips. Subcut remainder of 2 strips into 4 (4¾") F squares. Set aside remaining 3 strips for E borders.
- Cut 1 (11½" by fabric width) strip.
    Subcut strip into 2 (15½" x 11½") pillow back rectangles and 2 each 1½" x 11½" N strips and 1½" x 9½" M strips.
- Cut 5 (2¼" by fabric width) binding strips.

Completing the Quilt Top

Refer to the Assembly Diagram when piecing the quilt top.

1. Draw a diagonal line from corner to corner on the wrong side of each D square.

2. Place a D square on opposite corners of a C square with right sides together and stitch on the marked lines. Trim seam allowance to ¼" and press D to the right side as shown in Figure 1.

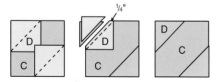

Figure 1

3. Repeat step 2 on the two remaining corners of C to complete one C-D unit as shown in Figure 2.

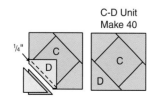

Figure 2

4. Repeat steps 2 and 3 to complete a total of 40 C-D units.

5. Select and join five C-D units and four B rectangles to make a sashing row; press seams toward B. Repeat to make a total of eight sashing rows.

6. Select and join four A squares with five B rectangles to make an A-B row; press seams toward B. Repeat to make a total of seven A-B rows.

7. Arrange and join the sashing rows with the A-B rows to complete the quilt center; press.

8. Join the E strips on the short ends to make a long strip; press. Subcut strip into two each 6½" x 44½" E strips.

9. Sew E strips to opposite long sides of the quilt center; press.

10. Sew a G triangle to each side of F to make a corner unit as shown in Figure 3; press. Repeat to make a total of four corner units.

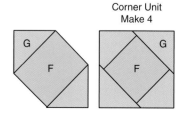

Figure 3

11. Sew a corner unit to opposite ends of each H strip.

12. Sew the pieced strips to the top and bottom of the quilt center to complete the quilt top; press.

Completing the Quilt

1. Sandwich the batting between the pieced top and a prepared backing piece; baste layers together. Quilt as desired.

2. When quilting is complete remove basting; trim batting and backing fabric even with raw edges of the pieced top.

3. Prepare binding and stitch to quilt front edges, matching raw edges, mitering corners and overlapping ends. Fold binding to back side and stitch in place to finish.

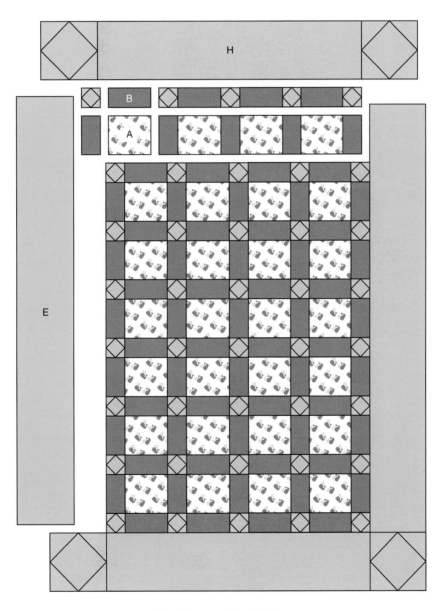

Rocking on the Water
Assembly Diagram 38" x 56"

Completing the Pillow Top

1. Prepare the whale motif for fusible appliqué and stitch to the I square referring to Raw-Edge Fusible Appliqué on page 15 and the Assembly Diagram for placement.

Designer's Quote

"The mini whale print fabric from Timeless Treasures inspired this cute little boy's quilt. The contemporary soft grays and blue are cool and refreshing." —Connie Kauffman

2. Draw a diagonal line from corner to corner on the wrong side of each J square.

3. Place a J square right sides together on opposite corners of I and stitch on the marked lines as shown in Figure 4.

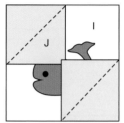

Figure 4

4. Trim excess beyond the stitched line to ¼" and press J to the right side as shown in Figure 5.

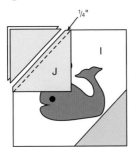

Figure 5

5. Repeat steps 3 and 4 on the remaining corners of I to complete the center unit as shown in Figure 6.

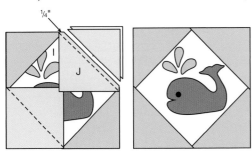

Figure 6

6. Sew K strips to the top and bottom, and L strips to opposite sides of the center unit; press.

7. Repeat step 6 with the M and N strips to complete the pillow top.

8. Using a mug, round the corners of the pillow top as shown in Figure 7.

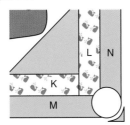

Figure 7

Completing the Pillow

1. Sandwich the 15" square of batting between the pieced top and the 15" square of lining fabric; baste layers together. Quilt in the ditch of seams.

2. When quilting is complete, trim edges even.

3. Fold each pillow back rectangle with wrong sides together to make two 7¾" x 11½" double-layer rectangles; press.

4. Lay one rectangle on the second rectangle, overlapping folded edges until the layered unit measures 11½" square; baste together at overlapped edges to hold as shown in Figure 8.

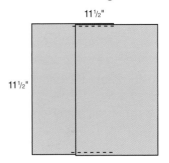

Figure 8

5. Place the quilted pillow top right sides together on top of the basted pillow back, matching edges; pin to hold. Trim pillow back corners even with pillow top.

6. Sew all around outer edges, securing seams at overlapped ends as shown in Figure 9.

Figure 9

7. Turn the pillow cover right side out through the back opening; press.

8. Stitch in the ditch of the seams between the M/K and N/L borders to form a flange on the edge as shown in Figure 10.

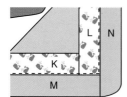

Figure 10

9. Place the two 9½" pillow form squares right sides together and stitch all around, leaving a 4" opening on one side. Turn right side out; press edges flat.

10. Insert polyester fiberfill through the opening to desired fullness.

11. Turn opening edges to the inside and hand-stitch opening closed to complete the pillow form.

12. Insert pillow form inside pillow cover through the back opening to finish. ●

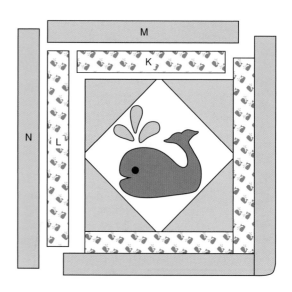

Rocking on the Water Pillow
Assembly Diagram 11" x 11"

Alternate Paper-Piecing Method

A paper-piecing pattern for the C-D units has been provided on the insert for those quilters who prefer precise piecing when working with small units.

1. Make 40 copies of the pattern given.

2. Cut 40 (2") blue tonal squares for piece 1.

3. Cut 80 (2") light gray tonal squares and cut each in half on one diagonal to make 160 triangles for pieces 2, 3, 4 and 5.

4. Stitch 40 C-D units using your favorite paper-piecing method.

Your Way

For a more traditional look, try using a collection of soft sherbet tonals or 1930s reproduction fabrics to create a scrappy and fun quilt that says, "Grandma made me."

Road to Bedtime

Three blocks, an interesting color palette and a weekend with your sewing machine, and you can have a keepsake quilt for one special toddler.

Designed & Quilted by Carolyn S. Vagts for The Village Pattern Co.

Skill Level

Confident Beginner

Finished Size

Quilt Size: 53" x 62"
Block Size: 9" x 9" finished
Number of Blocks: 30

Cutting

Prepare templates for appliqué using pattern given on the pattern insert. Cut pieces as per patterns, referring to Raw-Edge Fusible Appliqué on page 15.

From the 9 assorted tonal fat quarters:

- Cut 1 (5" x 21") strip each (9 strips total).
  Subcut strips into 4 (5") A squares each fabric
  (36 total).

Materials

- Multicolored batik scrap for howdah (seat)
- 9 assorted tonal fat quarters (blues, greens and purples used in the sample quilt)
- ½ yard each medium and dark gray tonals
- ⅔ yard mint green tonal
- 1⅔ yards white solid
- Backing to size
- Batting to size
- Thread
- 1½ yards fusible web
- 1¾ yards 20"-wide lightweight woven fusible interfacing
- Basic sewing tools and supplies

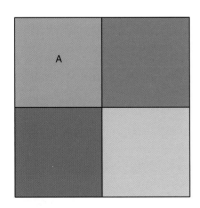

Four-Patch
9" x 9" Finished Block
Make 9

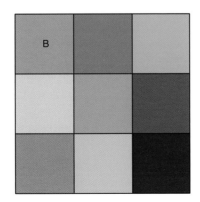

Nine-Patch
9" x 9" Finished Block
Make 9

Elephant
9" x 9" Finished Block
Make 12 (reverse 6)

- Cut 2 (3½" x 21") strips each (18 total). Subcut strips into 9 (3½") B squares each fabric (81 total).
- Cut remainder of fat quarters into 14 (2½" x 21") strips total for binding.

From mint green tonal:
- Cut 5 (1½" by fabric width) D/E strips.
- Cut 6 (1¼" by fabric width) H/I flange strips.

From white solid:
- Cut 3 (9½" by fabric width) strips. Subcut strips into 12 (9½") C squares.
- Cut 6 (3½" by fabric width) F/G strips.

From lightweight woven fusible interfacing:
- Cut 12 (9½") squares.

Completing the Four-Patch Blocks

1. Select four different-fabric A squares.

2. Join two A squares to make a row; repeat to make a second row.

3. Join the rows to complete one Four-Patch block as shown in Figure 1; press.

Figure 1

4. Repeat steps 1–3 to complete a total of nine Four-Patch blocks.

Completing the Nine-Patch Blocks

1. Select nine different-fabric B squares.

2. Arrange and join three B squares to make a B row; press. Repeat to make a total of three B rows.

3. Arrange and join the rows to complete one Nine-Patch block as shown in Figure 2; press.

Figure 2

4. Repeat steps 1–3 to complete a total of nine Nine-Patch blocks.

Completing the Elephant Blocks
Refer to Raw-Edge Fusible Appliqué on page 15 for all appliqué steps.

1. Fuse a 9½" square lightweight fusible interfacing to the wrong side of each C square.

2. Prepare shapes for six elephant and six reversed elephant fusible appliqué motifs.

3. Center and fuse an appliqué motif with pieces in numerical order onto one C square.

4. Machine-appliqué the elephant pieces in place using your favorite machine stitch and thread to match fabrics to complete one Elephant block.

5. Repeat steps 3 and 4 to complete a total of six Elephant blocks and six reversed Elephant blocks.

Completing the Quilt Top
Refer to the Assembly Diagram for positioning of blocks.

1. Arrange and join the Nine-Patch, Four-Patch and Elephant blocks in six rows of five blocks each; press.

2. Join the rows to complete the quilt center; press.

3. Join the D/E strips on the short ends to make a long strip; press. Subcut strip into two each 1½" x 54½" D strips and 1½" x 47½" E strips.

4. Sew D strips to opposite long sides and E strips to the top and bottom of the quilt center; press.

5. Join the F/G strips on the short ends to make a long strip; press. Subcut strip into two each 3½" x 56½" F strips and 3½" x 53½" G strips.

6. Sew F strips to opposite long sides and G strips to the top and bottom of the quilt center; press.

7. Join the H/I flange strips on the short ends to make a long strip; press. Subcut strip into two each 1¼" x 62½" H strips and 1¼" x 53½" I strips.

8. Fold the H and I strips in half with wrong sides together along the length to make double-layered flange strips; press. Set aside to apply after quilting is complete.

Completing the Quilt

1. Sandwich the batting between the pieced top and a prepared backing piece; baste layers together. Quilt as desired.

2. When quilting is complete remove basting; trim batting and backing fabric even with raw edges of the pieced top.

3. Pin and then baste an H flange strip to opposite long sides of the quilt center, matching outer raw edges as shown in Figure 3.

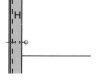

Figure 3

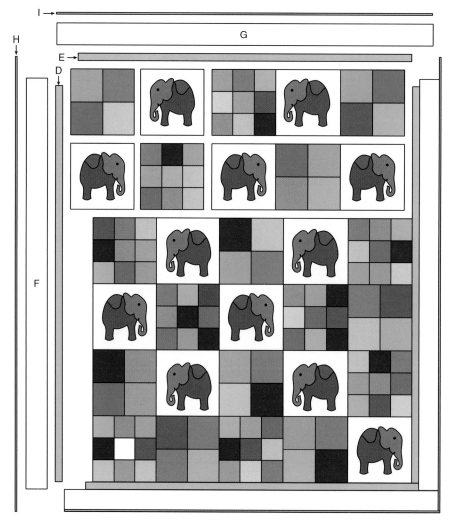

Road to Bedtime
Assembly Diagram 53" x 62"

4. Repeat step 3 with the I strips on the top and bottom, folding the corners at a 45-degree angle to simulate a mitered corner as shown in Figure 4.

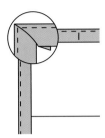

Figure 4

5. Prepare binding and stitch to quilt front edges, matching raw edges, mitering corners and overlapping ends. Fold binding to back side and stitch in place to finish. ●

Your Way

You can change the whole feel and appearance of Road to Bedtime simply by changing the color palette. Oranges, fuschias and a touch of yellow take this quilt in a totally different direction. This pattern would look great in almost any fabric.

Deep Blue Binkie

Turn your strips into an ocean of fun, add a fish or two, and you'll have a baby quilt that's not only beautiful but one that will also clean out that basket of fabric strips.

Designed & Quilted by Missy Shepler

Skill Level
Confident Beginner

Finished Size
Quilt Size: 40" x 40"

Materials
- 5" x 8" rectangle orange batik
- 4" x 8" rectangle orange batik
- 3½" x 6½" rectangle yellow batik
- 13 (1" x 32") blue/green strips
- 13 (1¼" x 32") blue/green strips
- 26 (1½" x 32") blue/green strips
- ⅜ yard blue tonal
- ½ yard sky fabric
- Backing to size
- Batting to size
- 5" x 8" rectangle thin batting
- Thread
- Black pearl cotton
- Basic sewing tools and supplies

Cutting
Prepare templates for pieced fish shapes using patterns given on insert. Cut as per patterns and instructions.

From blue tonal:
- Cut 5 (2¼" by fabric width) binding strips.

From sky fabric:
- Cut as per instructions.

Completing the Fish

1. Cut one each fish body from the 4" x 8" rectangle orange batik and fish belly from the 3½" x 6½" rectangle yellow batik using the prepared templates.

2. Pin the fish belly to the fish body matching dots at the ends of the seam and easing curved seams between dots; stitch to join the pieces as shown in Figure 1.

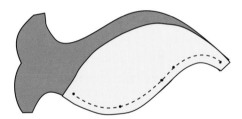

Figure 1

3. Clip into the curves and press the seam open to complete the pieced fish as shown in Figure 2.

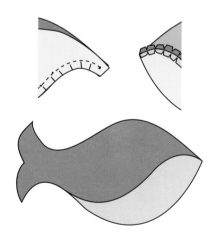

Figure 2

4. Using black pearl cotton, add a few straight stitches to make the eye as marked on pattern.

5. Pin the pieced fish shape right sides together with the 5" x 8" rectangle orange batik, adding thin batting on the bottom of the layers as shown in Figure 3.

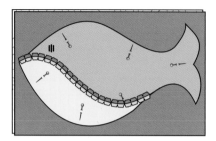

Figure 3

6. Cut around the fish shape through all layers as shown in Figure 4.

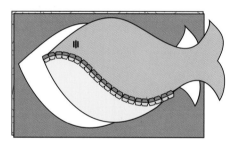

Figure 4

7. Stitch all around fish shape through all layers using a ¼" seam allowance, leaving a 3" opening on the top edge as shown in Figure 5.

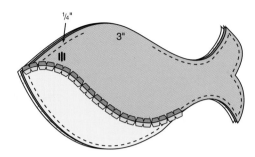

Figure 5

8. Referring to Figure 6, trim batting layer close to stitching and clip into seams on curved edges.

Figure 6

9. Turn the fish right side out through the opening; smooth edges flat at seams and press.

10. Turn opening edges to the inside; hand-stitch in place.

Adding a One-Piece Fish

If you prefer to make a one-color fish, use the one-piece fish pattern given in the insert. For this fish, you will need 2 (5" x 8") fabric rectangles—one for the fish shape and one for the backing shape—and 1 (5" x 8") thin batting rectangle.

1. Trace the fish shape onto one of the orange rectangles, layer with the remaining fabric and batting rectangles and stitch all around on the marked line, leaving a 2" opening on one side.

2. Cut out ⅛"–¼" beyond the stitching line and turn right side out through the opening. Press edges smooth and flat.

3. Turn opening edges to the inside and hand-stitch closed.

4. Add stitched details to the fish before applying to the surface of the quilt, if desired.

Completing the Quilt Top

Refer to the Placement Diagram when piecing the quilt top.

1. Select two 32"-long blue/green strips of any width and join along length; repeat with all strips to make strip pairs; press seams open.

2. Join the pairs along length into groups, pressing seams open. Join the groups to complete the pieced section.

3. Straighten one pieced edge of the pieced section.

4. Place the sky fabric right side up on a flat surface. Place the untrimmed edge of the pieced section right side up on the sky fabric with seams vertical, overlapping edges 6"–8" as shown in Figure 7. Pin layers together to hold.

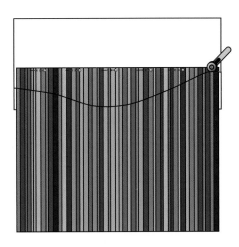

Figure 8

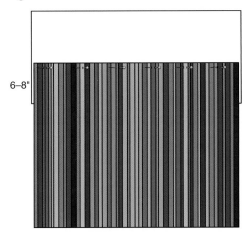

Figure 7

5. Using a fabric marker or tailor's chalk, draw a pleasing curved line across the pieced section within the overlapping area as shown in Figure 8.

6. When satisfied with the curving line, use a rotary cutter to cut along the line through both layers. Remove the cut part of the pieced section, leaving the trimmed layers flat as shown in Figure 9.

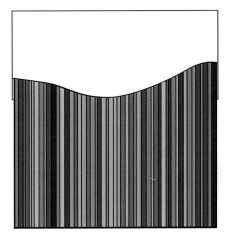

Figure 9

Here's a Tip

Sew up a school of fish and add dots of sewable hook-and-loop tape to the fish and the quilt to make a fun play quilt for little ones.

8. Flip the sky fabric piece right sides together with the pieced section and pin together at the alignment marks as shown in Figure 11.

Figure 11

9. Sew together, matching edges and using a ¼" seam allowance, being careful not to stretch the edge as you sew. Press seam toward the sky fabric.

10. Fold the stitched top in half to match top and bottom edges and trim side edges to make a 40½"-wide panel. Repeat the folding to match the trimmed sides and trim to complete the 40½"-tall pieced top.

Completing the Quilt

1. Sandwich the batting between the pieced top and a prepared backing piece; baste layers together. Quilt as desired.

2. When quilting is complete remove basting; trim batting and backing fabric even with raw edges of the pieced top.

3. Prepare binding and stitch to quilt front edges, matching raw edges, mitering corners and overlapping ends. Fold binding to back side and stitch in place.

4. Place the completed fish shape on the pieced section as desired. Hand-stitch in place through the center of the back side, catching the back of the fish and batting in the stitches to finish. ●

7. Draw alignment marks along the curved edge on both layers as shown in Figure 10. Remove excess sky fabric from beneath the layers.

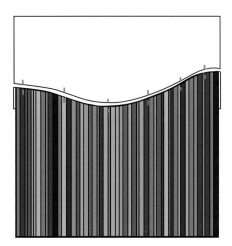

Figure 10

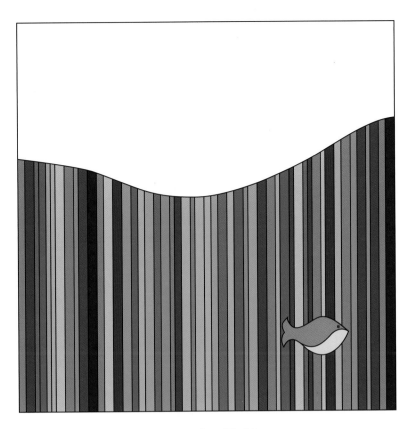

Deep Blue Binkie
Placement Diagram 40" x 40"

3-D Appliqué

Using 3-D appliqué in quilts adds interesting design details and dimension to a quilt. Usually the 3-D addition is a finished motif that is added to the surface of a finished quilt, such as a flower or other stand-alone motif.

The finished motif is not attached to the quilt's surface until after the quilting is complete because it would get caught up in the quilting, especially if the quilting is done by machine.

Once the quilting is complete, the 3-D motif is either hand- or machine-stitched to the surface of the quilt with care to avoid visible stitches on the back side of the quilt.

Your Way

For another fun color option try a grouping of grays, or maybe pinks or greens, and add bright fish for a pop of color.

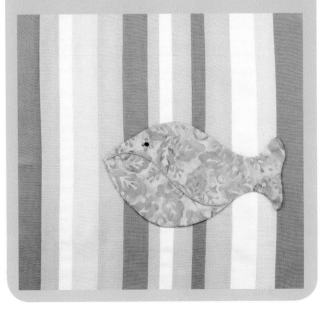

Special Thanks

Please join us in thanking the talented designers whose work is featured in this collection.

CJ Behling
Neopolitan Baby, page 27

Gina Gempesaw
Choo! Choo!, page 8

Connie Kauffman
Rocking on the Water, page 30

Chris Malone
Dotty Scotty, page 3

Missy Shepler
Rose Wall Quilt, page 16
Deep Blue Binkie, page 42

Carolyn S. Vagts for The Village Pattern Co.
Road to Bedtime, page 37

Robin Waggoner
Tutti Fruitti, page 23

Supplies

We would like to thank the following manufacturers who provided materials to make sample projects for this book.

Rocking on the Water, page 30: Whale print from Timeless Treasures, Soft & Bright batting from The Warm Company and PolyLite™ thread from Sulky of America.

Road to Bedtime, page 37: Quilting Temptations fabric collection from Quilting Treasures, Quilters Dream Puff batting and thread from Sulky of America.

Annie's® *Quick & Easy Baby Quilts* is published by Annie's, 306 East Parr Road, Berne, IN 46711. Printed in USA. Copyright © 2015 Annie's.

RETAIL STORES: If you would like to carry this publication or any other Annie's publication, visit AnniesWSL.com.

Every effort has been made to ensure that the instructions in this publication are complete and accurate. We cannot, however, take responsibility for human error, typographical mistakes or variations in individual work. Please visit AnniesCustomerService.com to check for pattern updates.

ISBN: 978-1-57367-664-9

1 2 3 4 5 6 7 8 9